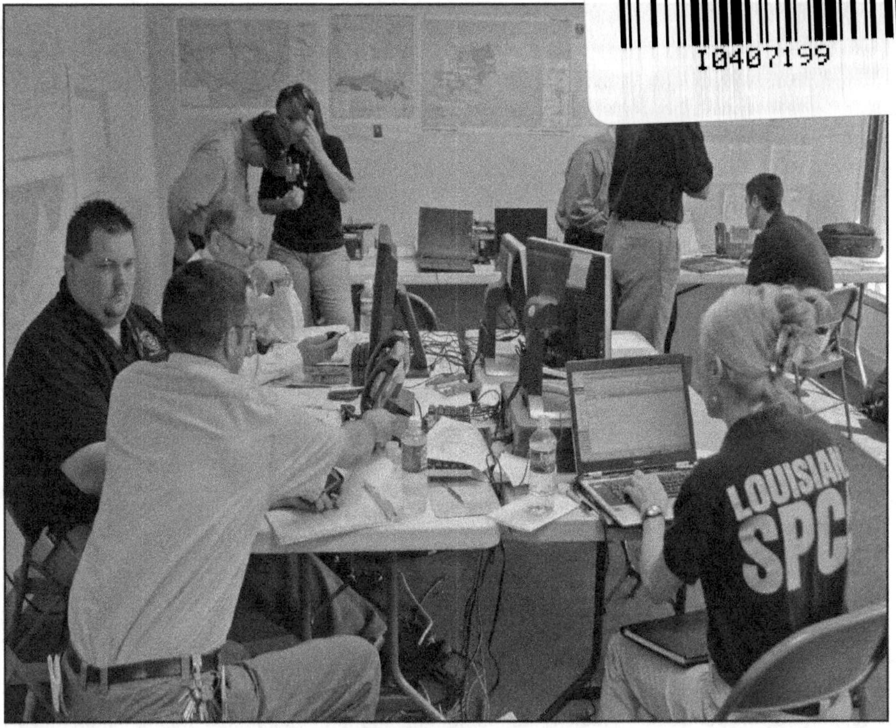

Decision Making and Problem Solving

Independent Study 241.a

May 2010

FEMA

Course Overview

About This Course

Being able to make decisions and solve problems effectively is a necessary and vital part of the job for every emergency manager, planner, and responder. This course is designed to improve your decision-making skills. It addresses:

- The decision-making process

- Decision-making styles

- Attributes of an effective decision maker

- Ethical decision making and problem solving

FEMA's Independent Study Program

The Federal Emergency Management Agency's (FEMA's) Independent Study Program is one of the delivery channels that the Emergency Management Institute (EMI) uses to provide training to the general public and specific audiences. This course is part of FEMA's Independent Study Program. In addition to this course, the Independent Study Program includes courses in floodplain management, radiological emergency management, the role of the emergency manager, hazardous materials, disaster assistance, the role of the Emergency Operations Center, and an orientation to community disaster exercises.

FEMA's independent study courses are available at no charge and include a final examination. You may apply individually or through group enrollment. When enrolling for a course, you must include your name, mailing address, social security number, and the title of the course in which you want to enroll.

FEMA's Independent Study Program

FEMA Independent Study Program
Administrative Office
Emergency Management Institute
16825 South Seton Avenue
Emmitsburg, MD 21727
(301) 447-1200

Information about FEMA's Independent Study Program also is available on the Internet at:

http://training.fema.gov/IS

Each request will be reviewed and directed to the appropriate course manager or program office for assistance.

Final Examination

This course includes a written final examination, which you must complete and return to FEMA's Independent Study Office for scoring. To obtain credit for taking this course, you must successfully complete (75 percent correct) this examination regardless of whether you complete this course through self-instruction or through group instruction.

You may take the final examination as many times as necessary.

Course Completion

The course completion deadline for all FEMA Independent Study courses is 1 year from the date of enrollment. The date of enrollment is the date that the EMI Independent Study Office will use for completion of all required course work, including the final examination. If you do not complete this course, including the final examination, within that timeframe, your enrollment will be terminated.

Decision Making and Problem Solving has no prerequisites.

How to Complete This Course

Work through this course at a pace that is comfortable for you. You should resist the temptation to rush through the material, however. Take enough time with each unit to ensure that you have mastered its content before proceeding to the next.

Knowledge Checks

To help you know when to proceed, each unit is followed by a Knowledge Check that addresses the material contained in the unit. The Knowledge Check asks you to answer questions that apply to what you have learned in the unit. The answers to the Knowledge Check follow each Knowledge Check.

When you finish each exercise, check your answers, and review the parts of the text that you do not understand. Do not proceed to the next unit until you are sure that you have mastered the current unit.

When you have completed all units, take the final examination online, or use the answer sheet (if provided in your course packet). EMI will score your test and notify you of the results.

Begin the Course

You may begin the course now.

Unit 1: Course Introduction

Introduction

Decision making and problem solving are critically important skill areas for emergency managers, planners, first responders, voluntary agency coordinators, and other professionals in emergency management.

As an emergency management professional, your ability to identify current and potential problems and to make sound, timely decisions before and during an emergency can literally affect the lives and well-being of the local citizenry. Your decisions can impact the ability of response agencies to do their jobs and can make the difference in how quickly the community is able to recover from an event.

Decisions in Emergency Management

How often are your decision-making abilities tested when an emergency threatens? Let's begin with an example. Review the case study that is provided on the next page.

Case Study 1.1—Sebring County

Instructions: Read the following case study. As you read, try to identify what decisions must be made by the emergency manager or other emergency management officials. Jot down your ideas before continuing.

Background: Heavy rainstorms have hit, and counties across the entire State are faced with flash flooding to varying degrees. The town of Westfield— located in Sebring County, one of the hardest hit counties in the State—sits high and well away from the river, so flooding is usually not a concern. Last year, a new spillway was built to increase the capacity of the town reservoir to about 44 million gallons. Two towns downstream, Ambry and Gilson, are less than a 5-minute drive from Westfield. Each town has about 2400 residents, most of them along U.S. Route 270.

Event chronology:

Late afternoon	Rain begins, and weather forecasters predict it will be a strong, slow-moving storm, which will produce heavy rain.
7:41 p.m.	A flash flood watch is issued by the National Weather Service.
8:00 p.m.	Heavy rains begin.
9:30 p.m.	The county engineer stations an employee on the dam to watch for and report any problems. The employee sees water pouring a good 2 feet over the spillway. (It was later estimated that the reservoir was holding 65 million gallons during and after the storm.)
11:00 p.m.	Five inches of rain have fallen over the last 3 hours.
12:30 a.m.	The employee sees a section of dirt break away.
1:00 a.m.	When water recedes below the top of the dam, county employees discover that water has eaten around the spillway and is gradually carving away the side of the earthen dam. A first attempt at closing the hole with sandbags fails when the force of the water carries the bags right through.
1:30 a.m.	The Sebring County Emergency Program Manager is now meeting with the mayor of Westfield, the county engineer, the public works director, the fire chief, and the police chief to discuss the situation.

Decision Points

What decision points did you identify in the case study? If you noted that the central problem is that if the dam breaks, the people in the downstream towns will be flooded, you're absolutely correct. Numerous decisions must be made to address this problem. Some of the key decisions that must be made are shown below, and you probably identified others as well.

- Should residents in the two downstream towns be evacuated?

- If the decision is to evacuate, when should the evacuation take place?

- Who will notify the citizens of the evacuation, and how?

- What additional resources will be necessary to accomplish the evacuation and provide any shelter needed?

- What is the most effective way to keep the dam from collapsing, and what resources will be needed to accomplish that?

What's At Stake?

The ability to make sound, timely decisions during an emergency event is critical. Good problem solving and decision making can avert tragedy and help the community recover from the event more quickly. Conversely, poor decision making—or the absence of decisions— potentially can result in injury or death to victims or responders. (Clearly, in our case study, if the Emergency Manager makes a poor decision—or simply doesn't make any decision before it's too late—the consequences could be disastrous for the residents of Ambry and Gilson.)

But the repercussions don't stop there. Poor decisions in the early stages of an event can make the responders' job more difficult and more dangerous. In addition, they can give rise to much more critical or complex decisions later on—to say nothing of the effect on community relations.

Good decision-making skills are one of your most critical assets as an emergency management professional. This course will help you develop those skills.

About This Course

Decision Making and Problem Solving contains six units. Each unit is described below.

- **Unit 1, Course Introduction,** provides an overview of the course.

- **Unit 2, The Decision-Making Process,** presents a five-step, problem-solving model and opportunities to apply the model to case studies. The unit also explores factors that affect decision making.

- **Unit 3, Identifying Decision-Making Styles and Attributes,** discusses the impact of personality type and personal preferences on decision-making style. During this unit, you will complete a personality type inventory and consider what that information indicates about your approach to decision making. This unit also explores what it takes to be an effective decision maker and what you can do to capitalize on your strengths and minimize your limitations.

- **Unit 4, Ethical Decision Making and Problem Solving,** focuses on situations involving ethical decisions and discusses the components of ethical decision making.

- **Unit 5, Decision Making in an Emergency,** gives you an opportunity to apply decision-making and problem-solving skills in a case study situation.

- **Unit 6, Course Summary,** summarizes key concepts from the entire course.

Activities and Exercises

This course will involve you actively as a learner by including activities and exercises that highlight basic concepts. It will also provide you with guidance on actions required in specific situations through the use of field-specific case studies.

Job Aids

Throughout the course, you will find job aids designed to guide you through a variety of decision-making tasks. They can be used during the course, and you will find them useful later, after you have completed the course.

Knowledge Checks

At the end of most units you will find a Knowledge Check. You can use these self-administered quizzes to verify that you have learned the content of the unit before moving on.

Appendix

In addition to the six units, this course includes an appendix that contains copies of all the job aids presented in the course.

Course Objectives

In *Decision Making and Problem Solving*, you will learn a decision-making model that can be used to make decisions and solve problems in both emergency and day-to-day situations. This self-paced course will provide you with a foundation of knowledge that will enable you to:

- Explain the need for decision-making and problem-solving skills in emergency management.

- Describe how decisions made before an emergency help the decision-making process during an emergency.

- Distinguish between a problem and its causes or symptoms.

- Analyze your personal attributes and relate them to your decision-making style.

- Describe the personal attributes of an effective decision maker.

- Explain how the ethics of a situation can affect decision making and problem solving.

- Apply a model for problem solving and decision making to emergency management scenarios.

How Will You Benefit?

You will benefit in several ways by taking this course:

- You will learn how to identify a problem—as distinguished from its causes or symptoms. Failure to identify the problem properly is one of the main reasons for poor decision making.

- You will learn a model for problem solving—and learn how to apply the model as a way of improving your decision making.

- You will become more aware of your own personal attributes as a decision maker and use that awareness as a starting point for improving your decision-making ability.

How To Complete This Course

This course is designed so that you can complete it on your own at your own pace. Take a break after each unit, and give yourself time to think about the material, particularly how it applies to your work as an emergency management professional and the decision-making situations you have encountered or anticipate encountering on the job.

Remember to complete the <u>activities and case study exercises</u> that are presented during the course. These activities and exercises emphasize different learning points, so be sure to complete all of them. Compare your answers to the answers provided following each activity or exercise. If your answers are correct, continue on with the material. If any of your answers are wrong, go back and review the material before continuing.

Take the short Knowledge Check quizzes at the end of Units 2 through 5. Check your answers using the answer key that follows each Knowledge Check. If you missed any questions, go back and review the material again.

After you have completed all of the units, complete the <u>final examination</u> that is available online through the Emergency Management Institute's Independent Study office, using the supplied answer sheet. To obtain credit for taking this course, you must successfully complete this examination (75 percent correct). EMI will score your test and notify you of the results. You may take the final examination as many times as necessary.

Sample Learning Schedule

Complete this course at your own pace. You should be able to finish the entire course—including pretest, units, Knowledge Checks, and Final Examination—in approximately 6 or 7 hours. The following learning schedule is only an example, intended to show relative times devoted to each unit.

Unit	Suggested Time
Unit 1: Course Introduction	1 hour
Unit 2: The Decision-Making Process	1 hour
Unit 3: Identifying Decision-Making Styles and Attributes	1 hour 45 minutes
Unit 4: Ethical Decision Making and Problem Solving	1 hour
Unit 5: Decision Making in an Emergency	1 hour
Unit 6: Course Summary	30 minutes

Goal Setting

What do you hope to gain through completing *Decision Making and Problem Solving*? Depending on your role in emergency management, your prior experience in decision-making and problem solving situations, and your current level of expertise in these areas, your goals may be slightly different from those of another emergency management professional.

Clarifying your goals will help you gain the most from the time you spend completing this course. Take a few minutes to complete the following activity.

Activity: Personal Learning Goals

Purpose: The purpose of this activity is to develop personal goals for this course.

Instructions:
1. Consider the following information:

   - The course objectives.
   - The potential benefits of completing this course.
   - Your own decision-making experience. Reflect on emergencies in which you have participated, the decisions that were made during those emergencies, and the consequences of those decisions. What have you learned—either positive or negative—from those experiences?

2. Think about what you would like to accomplish through this course. Then list three (or more) personal goals for improving your decision-making and problem-solving skills.

Goals

1. _____

2. _____

3. _____

Summary and Transition

In this unit, you previewed the course and considered your own goals for improving your decision-making and problem-solving skills. Unit 2 discusses the decision-making process.

Unit 2: The Decision-Making Process

Introduction

Whether making ordinary day-to-day decisions or critical, time-sensitive decisions in an emergency, using a standard problem-solving model will help ensure that your decisions are rational and logical.

In this unit, you will learn a five-step, problem-solving model. After completing this unit, you should be able to:

- Describe how decisions made before an emergency affect decision making and problem solving during an emergency.

- Describe the steps in the problem-solving model.

- Review a case study and distinguish the problem from its causes and symptoms.

Problem Solving vs. Decision Making

To begin, let's clarify what we mean by *problem solving* and *decision making* and how they relate to one another.

- **Problem solving** is a set of activities designed to analyze a situation systematically and generate, implement, and evaluate solutions.

- **Decision making** is a mechanism for making choices at each step of the problem-solving process.

Decision making is part of problem solving, and decision making occurs at every step of the problem-solving process.

Where Does the Process Begin?

Emergency decisions have their beginnings well before any emergency strikes. Often the number, type, and magnitude of decisions and problems that must be addressed during an emergency are a direct outgrowth of decisions that were (or weren't) made at the outset of the emergency, or even before the emergency began.

The following case study illustrates how early decisions can affect later decisions. Read the case study. Then, analyze the decision to determine how it might affect later decisions.

Case Study 2.1—Mandatory or Voluntary Evacuation?

The town of Fort Rice, North Dakota is located on the western bank of the Missouri River. A farming and ranching community, Fort Rice's residents are known for their tenacity in fighting the weather—and the river—to earn a living.

It has been raining for 12 hours, and the National Weather Service has forecast severe flooding conditions through most of the upper Midwest. The Missouri River and the rivers and streams that feed it are on the rise and are expected to continue to rise over the next several days as the storm is held in place by a large high-pressure area that is currently stationary over the Ohio Valley. Despite the fact that sandbagging crews have been supporting all local levees, severe flooding is a near certainty.

The mayor and all emergency management professionals from Fort Rice have been keeping abreast of the situation since before the rain began. They have been communicating with the local Weather Forecast Office, as well as county and State emergency management personnel. The question on the table at this point is not whether to issue an evacuation order but whether to make the evacuation mandatory.

Historically, farmers and ranchers have been unwilling to evacuate, even when flooding is severe. Most have grown up in the area and are aware of the damage that flooding can cause, but they are also aware of their investment in their land and livestock and will fight to save what they can.

After considerable discussion, the mayor, with the emergency management group's concurrence, makes the decision to activate the Emergency Alert System and issue the evacuation order. But although they decide to word the message strongly, they do not make the evacuation mandatory.

 **Case Study 2.1—Mandatory or Voluntary Evacuation? (Continued)**

Answers to the Case Study

<u>What is the potential impact of the decision not to make the evacuation mandatory</u>?

The early decision to issue an evacuation order but to not make it mandatory can seriously affect later decisions. Some of the ways in which later decisions can be affected are listed below. You may have additional examples as well.

- Farmers and ranchers who choose not to evacuate now may be in a position of needing to evacuate later, when evacuation will be more dangerous or impossible. How will the decision about how and when to effect an emergency rescue be made?
- Emergency responders who may later be required to assist with emergency rescues will be placed at risk. Who will make the decision to send responders into the fast-moving waters? When will that decision be made?
- Response resources deployed for emergency rescues may cause resource shortfalls elsewhere. How does one weigh the overall benefit of deploying resources for emergency rescues versus the cost of those resources not being available for other purposes (which may also involve life-saving efforts)?
- The overall cost for the response will increase if response resources must be deployed to assist with emergency rescues. While cost will not be an issue where the potential loss of life is involved, the decision not to require evacuation will affect later decisions about how to cover the overall costs of the emergency.

The Starting Point

As an emergency management professional, you have at your disposal a variety of resources designed to guide your decision making during emergencies.

When a jurisdiction develops an Emergency Operations Plan (EOP), Standard Operating Procedures (SOPs), or other procedural documents, it provides the foundation for decision making that will occur during emergencies.

Many decisions are made during the development of these documents, and there are real advantages to having made those decisions during the planning process rather than in the heat of an emergency.

- Decisions made under non-emergency conditions can be made deliberately, without the stress factors that accompany crisis decisions.

- Absence of critical time factors permits the jurisdiction to use group process, gather input from all of the involved parties, and achieve group consensus.

- The planning process allows enough time to consider all contingencies and weigh alternative responses fully.

- Planning in advance gives the jurisdiction time to obtain "buy-in" from the many stakeholders, to train and exercise the plan, and to educate the public about what to expect—and what to do—in an emergency.

The Starting Point (Continued)

Clearly, if your jurisdiction has an Emergency Operations Plan and procedures in place, that is the place to start your decision-making process when an emergency threatens or occurs. It will answer many questions, such as:

- Who is responsible for what? Who makes decisions?

- What organization should be used during response and recovery?

- What triggers each kind of action?

- How does communication take place?

- Under what conditions is evacuation initiated?

- What provisions are there for mass care?

As you implement the EOP, you can use the problem-solving model that is included later in this unit at any stage of an emergency response to ensure that you have the greatest possible control over the situation.

Mandates: Incident Management and Coordination Systems

On February 28, 2003, the President issued Homeland Security Presidential Directive 5 (HSPD–5), "Management of Domestic Incidents," which directed the Secretary of Homeland Security to develop and administer a National Incident Management System (NIMS). This system provides a consistent nationwide template to enable Federal, State, tribal, and local governments, nongovernmental organizations (NGOs), and the private sector to work together to prevent, protect against, respond to, recover from, and mitigate the effects of incidents, regardless of cause, size, location, or complexity. This consistency provides the foundation for utilization of NIMS for all incidents, ranging from daily occurrences to incidents requiring a coordinated Federal response.

The terrorist attacks of September 11, 2001, illustrated the need for all levels of government, the private sector, and nongovernmental agencies to prepare for, protect against, respond to, and recover from a wide spectrum of events that exceed the capabilities of any single entity. These events require a unified and coordinated national approach to planning and to domestic incident management. To address this need, the President signed a series of Homeland Security Presidential Directives (HSPDs) that were intended to develop a common approach to preparedness and response. Two HSPDs are of particular importance in effective decision making for your jurisdiction:

National Incident Management System (NIMS)

NIMS is not an operational incident management or resource allocation plan. NIMS represents a core set of doctrines, concepts, principles, terminology, and organizational processes that enables effective, efficient, and collaborative incident management.

Building on the foundation provided by existing emergency management and incident response systems used by jurisdictions, organizations, and functional disciplines at all levels, NIMS integrates best practices into a comprehensive framework for use nationwide by emergency management/response personnel in an all-hazards context. These best practices lay the groundwork for the components of NIMS and provide the mechanisms for the further development and refinement of supporting national standards, guidelines, protocols, systems, and technologies. NIMS fosters the development of specialized technologies that facilitate emergency management and incident response activities, and allows for the adoption of new approaches that will enable continuous refinement of the system over time.

NIMS (Continued)

According to the National Integration Center, "institutionalizing the use of ICS" means that government officials, incident managers, and emergency response organizations at all jurisdictional levels adopt the Incident Command System. Actions to institutionalizing ICS takes place at two levels—policy and organizational/operational:

At the policy level, institutionalizing ICS means government officials:

- Adopt ICS through executive order, proclamation or legislation as the jurisdiction's official incident response system.

- Direct that incident managers and response organizations in their jurisdictions train, exercise, and use ICS in their response operations.

At the organizational/operational level, incident managers and emergency response organizations should:

- Integrate ICS into functional, system-wide emergency operations policies, plans, and procedures.

- Provide ICS training for responders, supervisors, and command-level officers.

- Conduct exercises for responders at all levels, including responders from all disciplines and jurisdictions.

NIMS integrates existing best practices into a consistent, nationwide approach to domestic incident management that is applicable at all jurisdictional levels and across functional disciplines.

NIMS (Continued)

Five major components make up the NIMS system approach:

- **Preparedness:** Effective emergency management and incident response activities begin with a host of preparedness activities conducted on an ongoing basis, in advance of any potential incident. Preparedness involves an integrated combination of assessment; planning; procedures and protocols; training and exercises; personnel qualifications, licensure, and certification; equipment certification; and evaluation and revision.

- **Communications and Information Management:** Emergency management and incident response activities rely on communications and information systems that provide a common operating picture to all command and coordination sites. NIMS describes the requirements necessary for a standardized framework for communications and emphasizes the need for a common operating picture. This component is based on the concepts of interoperability, reliability, scalability, and portability, as well as the resiliency and redundancy of communications and information systems.

- **Resource Management:** Resources (such as personnel, equipment, or supplies) are needed to support critical incident objectives. The flow of resources must be fluid and adaptable to the requirements of the incident. NIMS defines standardized mechanisms and establishes the resource management process to identify requirements, order and acquire, mobilize, track and report, recover and demobilize, reimburse, and inventory resources.

- **Command and Management:** The Command and Management component of NIMS is designed to enable effective and efficient incident management and coordination by providing a flexible, standardized incident management structure. The structure is based on three key organizational constructs: the Incident Command System, Multiagency Coordination Systems, and Public Information.

- **Ongoing Management and Maintenance:** Within the auspices of Ongoing Management and Maintenance, there are two components: the National Integration Center (NIC) and Supporting Technologies.

Additional information about NIMS can be accessed online at www.fema.gov/emergency/NIMS or by completing EMI's IS 700 online course.

National Response Framework (NRF)

The NRF is a guide to how the Nation conducts all-hazards response – from the smallest incident to the largest catastrophe. This key document establishes a comprehensive, national, all-hazards approach to domestic incident response. The Framework identifies the key response principles, roles, and structures that organize national response. It describes how communities, States, the Federal Government, and private-sector and nongovernmental partners apply these principles for a coordinated, effective national response.

The NRF is:

- **Always in effect, and elements can be implemented as needed on a flexible, scalable basis to improve response.** It is not always obvious at the outset whether a seemingly minor event might be the initial phase of a larger, rapidly growing threat. The NRF allows for the rapid acceleration of response efforts without the need for a formal trigger mechanism.

- **Part of a broader strategy.** The NRF is required by, and integrates under, a larger National Strategy for Homeland Security that:

  - Serves to guide, organize, and unify our Nation's homeland security efforts.

  - Reflects our increased understanding of the threats confronting the United States.

  - Incorporates lessons learned from exercises and real-world catastrophes.

  - Articulates how we should ensure our long-term success by strengthening the homeland security foundation we have built.

- **Comprised of more than the core document.** The NRF is comprised of the core document, the Emergency Support Function (ESF), Support, and Incident Annexes, and the Partner Guides. The core document describes the doctrine that guides our national response, roles and responsibilities, response actions, response organizations, and planning requirements to achieve an effective national response to any incident that occurs.

NRF (Continued)

The following documents provide more detailed information to assist practitioners in implementing the Framework:

- **Emergency Support Function Annexes** group Federal resources and capabilities into functional areas that are most frequently needed in a national response (e.g., Transportation, Firefighting, Search and Rescue).

- **Support Annexes** describe essential supporting aspects that are common to all incidents (e.g., Financial Management, Volunteer and Donations Management, Private-Sector Coordination).

- **Incident Annexes** address the unique aspects of how we respond to seven broad incident categories (e.g., Biological, Nuclear/Radiological, Cyber, Mass Evacuation).

Additional information about the NRF can be accessed online at www.fema.gov/emergency/NRF or by completing EMI's IS 800.b online course.

What These Changes Mean to You

Your jurisdiction is required to:

- Use NIMS to manage all incidents, including recurring and/or planned special events.

- Integrate all response agencies and entities into a single, seamless system, from the Incident Command Post, through department Emergency Operations Centers (DEOCs) and local Emergency Operations Centers (EOCs), through the State EOC to the regional- and national-level entities.

- Develop and implement a public information system.

- Identify and type all resources according to established standards.

- Ensure that all personnel are trained properly for the job(s) they perform.

- Ensure communications interoperability and redundancy.

Remember the importance of working with VOADs, NGOs, business and industry, and others to develop a plan for addressing volunteer needs *before* an emergency to help eliminate some of the potential problems that can occur *during* an emergency.

Problem-Solving Model

There are many different decision-making/problem-solving models that you can use. The five-step model shown below has proven effective in emergency situations. When using this model, each step may be completed quickly, but every step must be considered. It is not necessary to document each step, but it is important to think through every step.

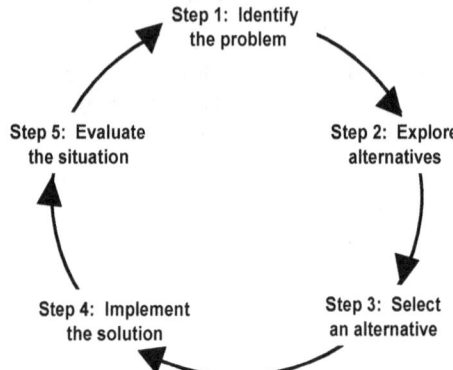

Step 1: Identify the problem

Step 2: Explore alternatives

Step 3: Select an alternative

Step 4: Implement the solution

Step 5: Evaluate the situation

In the remainder of this unit, we will take a closer look at each of the five steps and how you can apply them to emergencies.

Step 1. Identify the Problem

Problem identification is undoubtedly the most important—and the most difficult—step in the process. All subsequent steps will be based on how you define and assess the problem at hand.

What Is a "Problem"?

A **problem** is a situation or condition of people or the organization that will exist in the future, and that is considered undesirable by members of the organization.

Problem or Solution?

In carrying out Step 1, you must distinguish between a *problem* and its *solution*. The most common error in problem solving is defining problems in terms of their solutions. Sometimes people think that they are articulating problems when actually they are stating a potential solution.

Here's an example: Someone might say, "The problem is that we don't have an EOC." The problem, however, is not that there is no EOC.

- The problem is really that the emergency management community cannot coordinate communications adequately during the response phase.

- Establishing an EOC is a solution.

Delineating the Problem Parameters

Identifying the problem also involves analyzing the situation to determine the extent of the problem. Problem parameters include:

- What is happening (and is not happening).

- Who is involved.

- What the stakes are.

On the next page is a Checklist for Identifying, Defining, and Analyzing Problems. The checklist presents a set of questions that can help you define a problem accurately. (This job aid is also provided in the Appendix for easy reference at a later time.)

Step 1 Job Aid: Checklist for Identifying, Defining, and Analyzing Problems

Question	Yes	No
1. Is this a new problem?	☐	☐
2. Is the problem clearly and precisely stated?	☐	☐
3. What assumptions am I making about the problem? Are they true?	☐	☐
4. What would happen if <u>nothing</u> were done about this problem?		
5. Can the problem be restated in other terms? If yes, how?	☐	☐
6. What <u>data</u> are known that bear on the problem?		

Step 1 Job Aid: Checklist for Identifying, Defining, and Analyzing Problems (Continued)

Question	Yes	No
7. Is the information accurate?	☐	☐
8. Are there any precedents or rules about other procedures that apply to the problem? If so, what precedents or rules apply?	☐	☐
9. What additional facts are needed to analyze the problem? (List)		
10. Is it possible to interpret the facts differently? How would that affect the problem's solution?	☐	☐
11. Do I have to make this decision, or does someone else? If this decision is someone else's to make, whose is it?	☐	☐

Step 2. Explore Alternatives

The second step in the decision-making process is to explore alternative solutions to the problem identified in Step 1. This step really consists of two parts:

- Generating alternatives

- Evaluating alternatives

The case study presented below provides an opportunity to examine a problem and generate alternative solutions. Read the case study, then identify the problem and generate as many alternative solutions as you can.

Case Study 2.2—What Are Your Options?

Auburn, Maine is a city of 24,000 located on the Androscoggin River, 50 miles north of Portland. Like much of southern Maine, Auburn has a growing population of retirees and elderly persons, many of whom reside in assisted-living communities.

It is early December, and much of southwestern Maine has been under the influence of a low-pressure system. Unlike most nor'easters that occur regularly this time of year, however, this system features warm air aloft with below-freezing surface temperatures. Thus, the rain that is falling is freezing on roads, trees, and electric lines. Electricity has been interrupted to a large portion of the city as wires collapse under the increasing weight of the accumulating ice.

At 11:00 p.m., the local emergency manager receives a call forwarded from emergency dispatch stating that the Owl's Nest nursing home's generator has failed. Owl's Nest is a nursing home, assisted-living community of approximately 250 residents. Of those, approximately 80 have been affected by the generator failure. These patients are in the nursing home portion of the facility, and many are chronically ill and very susceptible to the effects of the cold and dampness. For now, the Owl's Nest administrator has gathered the affected residents in the recreation room and is using blankets to keep them warm. This is not a good long-term option, however, because the temperature is expected to drop into the teens by morning.

Case Study 2.2—What Are Your Options? (Continued)

Answers to the Case Study

<u>What is the problem in this case study</u>?

If you determined that the problem in this case study centers around how to keep the nursing home residents warm, your answer is correct. (Note: If your problem statement centers on either the weather or the failed generator, please review the problem identification section of this unit again. Both the weather and the failed generator are <u>causes</u> of the current problem.)

<u>What alternatives are available</u>?

Some of the options that you may have developed for this case study could be:

- Evacuate the affected residents to another portion of the facility or to a shelter.
- Bring in more blankets, hot drinks, etc., to keep the residents warm.
- Bring in a portable generator and commercial space heaters.

You may have developed other alternatives as well. Remember, at this point in the problem-solving process, you should be generating alternatives only, not evaluating the feasibility of the alternatives.

Step 2. Explore Alternatives (Continued)

Techniques for Generating Alternatives

So, what process did you use to generate the alternatives for the case study? There are three ways to generate alternatives.

- **Brainstorming** can be done individually or in a group. Brainstorming requires an environment in which the participants (individuals or group members) are free to "think out loud." Participants blurt out as many ideas as possible within a specified time period. No evaluation of ideas is permitted so as to encourage the free flow of creative ideas. These ideas are recorded. When the specified time period ends, then evaluation of the ideas begins.

- **Surveys** economically tap the ideas of a large group of respondents. Surveys present respondents with the problem and a series of alternative solutions.

- **Discussion groups** should consist of those who are directly involved in decision making. In generating alternatives, the group members should:

  - Be comprehensive.
  - Avoid initial judgments (as in brainstorming).
  - Focus on the problem, not on the personalities of the people involved in the decision-making process. (But be sensitive to the impact of personalities on the process.)

Criteria for Evaluating Alternatives

After you have generated alternative solutions, you must have some means of evaluating them. Step 2 Job Aid lists criteria by which you can evaluate alternatives.

Another part of evaluation is identifying contingencies—what could go wrong. Think in terms of Murphy's Law ("If anything can go wrong, it will.") and identify what could get in the way of solving the problem you are facing.

Step 2 Job Aid: Criteria for Evaluating Alternatives

Step	Questions to Ask
1. Identify Constraints	Do any of the following factors serve as a limitation on this solution? • Technical (limited equipment or technology) • Political (legal restrictions or ordinances) • Economic (cost or capital restrictions) • Social (restrictions imposed by organized groups with special interests) • Human resources (limited ability of relevant people to understand or initiate certain actions) • Time (requirements that a solution be found within a prescribed time period, thereby eliminating consideration of long-range solutions)
2. Determine Appropriateness	Does this solution fit the circumstances?
3. Verify Adequacy	Will this option make enough of a difference to be worth doing?
4. Evaluate Effectiveness	Will this option meet the objective?
5. Evaluate Efficiency	What is the cost/benefit ratio of this option?
6. Determine Side Effects	What are the ramifications of this option?

Step 3. Select an Alternative

The third step in the problem-solving model is to select one of the alternatives explored in Step 2 for implementation. After you have evaluated each alternative, one should stand out as coming closest to solving the problem with the most advantages and fewest disadvantages.

Implementing the solution may not be easy, however. There may be repercussions, and you should complete a "reality check" to identify and evaluate the possible consequences of implementing the solution. Carefully consider how the solution will be implemented before selecting an alternative.

Selecting an alternative is a critical step in the problem-solving process. Review the previous case study (presented again below) and select the best alternative from the list that you developed in the previous activity.

When selecting an alternative, you will encounter factors that affect your decision making. These factors may include:

- Political factors.

- Safety factors.

- Financial factors.

- Environmental considerations.

- Ethical factors (more about ethical factors in Unit 4).

Not all of these factors may be readily recognizable. As you examine the situation and apply the problem-solving model, be alert for these potential limits on the solutions that you can implement.

Step 3 Job Aid: Best Solutions

Solution:		
Limiting Factors:		
Political:		
Safety:		
Financial:		
Environmental:		
Ethical:		
Other:		

Solution:		
Limiting Factors:		
Political:		
Safety:		
Financial:		
Environmental:		
Ethical:		
Other:		

Solution:		
Limiting Factors:		
Political:		
Safety:		
Financial:		
Environmental:		
Ethical:		
Other:		

If you have more than one clear solution, can any be combined?

Step 4. Implement the Solution

The fourth step involves five subparts.

- **Develop an action plan.** Implementation requires a series of steps to:

  - Articulate who has to do what, with what resources, by what time, and toward what goal.
  - Identify who must know about the decision.

  Step 4 Job Aid, the Action Planning Checklist, on the following page will help you to plan the details needed for implementation.

- **Determine objectives.** Objectives are measurable targets that are:

  - Used to monitor progress and establish priorities.
  - Based on analysis of the situation and contingencies.

- **Identify needed resources.** Resources include people, information (data), and things. Ask yourself:

  - What resources do I need?
  - Where will I get them?
  - How long will it take?
  - What can others offer?
  - Are there any special requirements?

- **Build a plan.** Your plan should state:

  - Who ...
  - Will do what (and with whom) ...
  - By when
  - Where
  - How

  Remember: Communicate the plan to all parties involved!

- **Implement the plan.** Use the action plan to put the decision in place.

Activity: Implementing the Solution

This activity will give you an opportunity to develop an action plan for the solution you selected for the previous case study. Follow the steps below to complete this activity:

1. Print or copy the Step 4 Job Aid. This job aid appears in Appendix A, page 5.

2. Use the job aid to develop a basic action plan to implement the solution you selected in Step 3 of this unit.

3. Don't worry if you can't provide all of the details for the action plan. The point of this activity is for you to consider all of the many factors involved in implementing the solution you chose.

Step 4 Job Aid: Action Planning Checklist

Use the following questions to help you develop any details needed to plan for implementation of the decision.

1. Will the decision be implemented as it stands or will it have to be modified?

    ☐ As it stands
    ☐ With modifications (List)

2. Does the decision fit the problem and conditions specified earlier?

    ☐ Yes
    ☐ No

3. Is this still the best option?

    ☐ Yes
    ☐ No

    (If no, what has changed?)

4. What are the side effects of this decision?

5. Who is responsible for taking action?

Step 4 Job Aid: Action Planning Checklist (Continued)

6. Are the specific targets to be accomplished and the techniques for accomplishing them defined?

   ☐ Yes
   ☐ No

   If no, what targets and techniques required further definition?

7. What specific activities must take place to implement this decision? In what sequence?

8. What resources will be needed to implement this decision?

9. What is the schedule or timetable for implementation of each step in the action plan?

Activity: Implementing the Solution (Continued)

The correct answers are:

Again, there is no single correct answer to this activity. Your answer is correct if your action plan:

- Presents the best of the feasible solutions.
- Addresses foreseeable side effects.
- Identifies who will take the action.
- Describes the activities required to implement the solution.
- Describes the resources needed to implement the solution.
- Includes a timetable for implementing the solution.

Remember that the plan must be disseminated to all who have responsibility for any part of implementing it.

Step 5. Evaluate the Situation

Evaluation involves two parts:

- **Monitoring progress.** Ask:

  - Has the situation changed?
  - Are more (or fewer) resources required?
  - Is a different alternative solution required?

  Monitoring the success and results of a decision is an ongoing process that is critical to fine tuning a course of action.

- **Evaluating the results.** Use the following checklist to help you evaluate the decision.

Step 5 Job Aid: Checklist for Evaluating the Results

Use the questions below as a guide for evaluating the results of your decision making.

Question	Yes	No
1. How will you know if the proposed decision has worked? Is it measurable? If yes, how?	☐	☐
2. Does the decision and action plan make use of existing channels of communication to generate feedback?	☐	☐
3. Will the feedback test the effectiveness of the decision?	☐	☐
4. Will the feedback be sufficient to reflect changing circumstances and conditions that might occasion the need to modify the plan?	☐	☐
5. Is the solution achieving its purpose?	☐	☐
6. Is timely information generated so that it can be supplied to operational, administrative, and policy units in the jurisdiction?	☐	☐

Activity: Evaluating Your Solution

This activity will provide an opportunity for you to determine how you would evaluate the solution that you selected in response to the previous case study. Follow the steps below to complete this activity:

1. Print or copy Step 5 Job Aid.

2. Using the job aid, determine how you would evaluate the solution you selected in response to the case study. Consider each of the factors above as you complete your evaluation.

3. Don't worry if you can't answer each of the questions on the job aid. The point of this activity is to understand that the problem-solving process is not complete unless the solution implemented is evaluated and the evaluation data are fed back into the process.

Activity: Evaluating Your Solution (Continued)

The correct answers are:

There is no single correct answer to this activity. Your answer is correct if it:

1. Clearly identifies benchmarks or measures that will indicate to you whether or not the solution is working.

2. Generates feedback from those who are charged with implementing the solution (or are affected by it) and if that feedback:

- Reflects the effectiveness of the decision.
- Indicates whether or not the solution is achieving its purpose.
- Is timely and can be fed back into operational, administrative, and policy units.

Summary and Transition

In Unit 2 you examined the decision-making process, including a 5-step problem-solving model. Unit 3 will examine different decision-making styles and attributes.

For More Information

National Incident Management System (NIMS):
http://www.fema.gov/emergency/nims/

National Response Framework (NRF):
http://www.fema.gov/emergency/nrf/

Knowledge Check

Select or provide the best answer. Turn the page to check your answers against the solutions.

1. Problem solving is part of decision making.

   a. True
   b. False

2. Number the five steps in the problem-solving model below in the correct order.

   _____ Explore alternatives.
   _____ Evaluate the solution.
   _____ Implement the solution.
   _____ Identify the problem.
   _____ Select an alternative.

3. Decision making before an emergency is not as effective because decision makers cannot anticipate all of the contingencies.

   a. True
   b. False

4. Criteria for evaluating alternatives include all of the following <u>except</u>:

   a. Ease
   b. Effectiveness
   c. Constraints
   d. Side effects

5. Step 4, Implement a Solution, involves all of the following <u>except</u>:

   a. Develop an action plan
   b. Determine objectives
   c. Identify needed resources
   d. Evaluate the results

Knowledge Check (Continued)

1. b (Decision making is part of problem solving.)
2. 2, 5, 4, 1, 3
3. b
4. a
5. d

Unit 3: Identifying Decision-Making Styles and Attributes

Introduction

In this unit, you will learn about the various styles of decision making. After completing this unit, you should be able to:

- Identify your psychological type and relate it to personal preferences.

- Describe factors and personal styles that have an impact on decision making.

- Distinguish between situations requiring individual decisions and those requiring group decisions.

- Identify the attributes of an effective decision maker.

- Determine your preferred decision-making style.

What Is Psychological Type?

A *psychological type* is a personality pattern based on the theory of psychiatrist Carl Jung. Based on his observation of people's behavior, Jung concluded that people have inherent differences in how they use their minds and where they derive and focus their energy.

Jung identified two mental processes:

- Taking in information (or perceiving).

- Organizing information and drawing conclusions (or judging).

What Is Psychological Type? (Continued)

Jung also identified two different ways in which people do each of these mental activities:

- People take in information either through their senses or by intuition.
- People organize information either by thinking or by feeling.

People also differ in where they derive and focus their energy. They are either externally oriented (extroverts), energized by people and activity; or internally oriented (introverts), energized by ideas and thoughts.

These different ways of organizing and relating to the world obviously can be combined in different ways, thus creating different psychological types. For example, one person could be an extrovert who relies on thinking more than feeling and sensing over intuiting, while another individual could be an introvert who is intuitive and feeling-oriented.

What Are Preferences?

Preferences are the *dominant* ways in which an individual functions. The following brief exercise illustrates what is meant by preferences.

Fold your hands. Note which thumb is on top. Now fold your hands so that the opposite thumb is on top. Did you notice that you naturally fold your hands one way, while the other required a bit more thought and effort? The natural way— the way you do it first, without thinking—is your preference. Notice that you were able to do the task the other way, but that it was not your preferred way.

Using Personality Assessments to Determine Preferences

One kind of personality inventory tool is the Myers-Briggs Type Indicator®. Log onto the MBTI® Web site: www.humanmetrics.com/cgi-win/JTypes2.asp and complete the inventory. Note your type and then continue with this unit.

Complete the assessment and review the feedback on expressed preferences. Remember, it is important to note that there are no right or wrong preferences. Each type has characteristic strengths and weaknesses. The point is to know yourself so that you can maximize your strengths, minimize or compensate for your weaknesses, and realize that your preferences affect the way you make decisions.

Preferences and Decision Making

Our preferences affect how we make decisions. For example, someone who is thinking-oriented will obviously have a different approach to decision making than someone who is feeling-oriented.

Your Type—What Does It Mean for Decision Making?

When you took the personality profile online, you received four letters indicating your preferred type (of two possible types) in each of four functions. The two middle letters (S or N, T or F) indicate your dominant decision-making type.

Each dominant function has its own characteristic strengths and blind spots when it comes to decision making. The following are some generalizations about each dominant function:

- **Sensing:** The bias is toward stability. Decisions have to make sense based on past experience. Asks, "What are the facts, costs, and benefits?"

- **Intuition:** The bias is toward innovation. Decisions should creatively make use of new opportunities and insights. Asks, "What are the patterns and possible interpretations?"

- **Thinking:** The bias is toward effectiveness. Decisions must be objective and logical. Asks, "What are the pros and cons, causes and effects?"

- **Feeling:** The bias is toward integrity. Decisions should consider people's values and needs. Asks, "How does this affect those involved?"

What Does It Mean to Flex?

A key to good decision making is that it uses both sensing and intuition to gather all the pertinent information, and both thinking and feeling to weigh all the factors involved. When we rely only on our dominant function, we tend to miss things and make poorer decisions.

To flex means to ask yourself the questions of the other three functions, as well as the questions of your dominant function that naturally occur to you. Although this process may feel awkward at first, it will lead to decisions that are more sound.

Activity: Where Should You Flex?

This activity will provide an opportunity to examine your preferred decision-making style as you interact with others. Follow the steps below to complete this activity:

1. Read Case Study 3.1, The Planning Meeting, on the next page.

2. Analyze the case study to determine points at which you would need to flex your preferences to ensure that the decision made is sound.

3. Think about this case study in terms of your preference. How would *you* have to flex if you were the emergency manager in this situation?

Activity: Where Should You Flex? (Continued)

Case Study 3.1
The Planning Meeting

Carl is the emergency manager for Howard County, Indiana. Howard County is a rural county that is located approximately 40 miles north of Indianapolis. The largest city in Howard County is Kokomo, which has a population of 45,000 and is the home of Indiana University at Kokomo. The remainder of Howard County is rural and includes the towns of New London, West Middleton, Alto, Center, Sycamore, Plevna, and Cassville.

The Howard County EOP is currently undergoing review, and Carl has gathered together the key players from Kokomo and all of the smaller towns so that the updated EOP accurately reflects the needs, resources, and capabilities of the entire county. Carl's goal is to gain buy-in from the key players, then train and exercise the plan as a team. This course seems absolutely logical to Carl because most of the communities in the county have mutual aid agreements and routinely assist each other during emergencies. The problem Carl sees is that, even though mutual aid agreements are in place, overall planning and coordination is lacking. Thus, when mutual aid agreements are activated, issues arise over who is in charge, what resources should be deployed, etc.

The meeting started amicably enough but differences soon became apparent. The fire chiefs from Alto and Middleton engaged in a heated discussion concerning calls in which both departments responded. Neither chief wanted to relinquish authority over his firefighters. Both believed that the firefighters were loyal to them and would perform better if the chains of command were kept separate. The Kokomo fire chief, whose department used ICS unified command in such situations, tried to intervene, but neither of the other chiefs would consider relinquishing authority.

Carl listened to the conversation for awhile, disbelieving the illogic of the chiefs' behavior. To him, the whole conversation was absurd. Of course, joint responses required a unified command structure.

1. Who should flex in this situation?

2. What is/are the key decision point(s) where flexibility is required in this case study?

3. Given what you can tell about Carl's preferences, how can Carl help to resolve the conflict?

 **Activity: Where Should You Flex? (Continued)**

Answers to the Planning Meeting Scenario

1. Who should flex in this situation?

   There is plenty of room for flexibility on the parts of both of the fire chiefs. ICS has been well proven to be effective in all kinds of responses; unfortunately, neither of the chiefs seems willing to budge.

   Carl could be setting himself up to be inflexible as well. He has already made the judgment that the chiefs' conversation is absurd. Given Carl's current position, if he tries to intervene into the situation, it will only escalate. In fact, Carl runs the risk of alienating both fire chiefs and losing their cooperation in the planning process.

2. What is/are the key decision point(s) where flexibility is required in this case study?

   One obvious decision point is whether or not the fire chiefs can reach agreement on using an ICS unified command on joint calls. A less obvious decision point is Carl's. What should he do to diffuse the situation?

3. Given what you know about Carl's preferences, how can Carl help to resolve the conflict?

   Carl's initial response suggests that he has strong preferences toward "S" (sensing), "T" (thinking), and "J" (judging). He needs to suspend judgment and work with the fire chiefs to see the situation from their individual points of view. By acting as a mediator, Carl can help both chiefs understand that by implementing a unified command, neither relinquishes authority but that decisions would be made as a team. By working together, the decisions made will help ensure the most effective response possible.

   Given Carl's initial response and his clear STJ preferences, the flexibility that he needs to show to resolve the issue may be "painful."

Who Decides?

In addition to the four dominant functions explained above, there are also four styles of decision making based on who makes the decision. As you read through the four styles, note that the amount of control that the leader has over the decision drops from total to almost none. Yet, the leader retains ultimate responsibility.

As an emergency manager, you work often in situations that require a high degree of coordination. These cases call for a group decision-making process. There are other times, however, when you must make a command decision alone. Several factors affect whether a decision should be made by an individual or a group. Use the questions in Job Aid 3-1, on the following page, to determine whether the circumstances call for an individual or group decision.

Individual Decision Making

In individual decision making, the leader must make the decision alone, and input from others is limited to collecting relevant information.

Decision Making Through Consultation

In consultation, the leader shares the issue with one or more people—seeking ideas, opinions, and suggestions—and then makes a decision. The leader considers the input of others, but the final decision may or may not be influenced by it.

Group Decision Making

In this case, the leader and others work together until they reach a consensus decision. Each group member's opinion and point of view is considered. As a result of helping to make the decision, group members buy into the final decision and commit to supporting its implementation.

Delegating the Decision

When delegating a decision, the leader sets the parameters, then allows one or more others to make the final decision. Although the leader does not make the decision, he or she supports it.

Job Aid 3-1: Selecting a Decision-Making Approach

Use the questions below as a guide to developing a decision-making approach. Answer each of the questions below.

- *If the response to question 1 is "No," it may be preferable to make the decision individually or in consultation with key players.*
- *If the response to question 2 is "No," it may be preferable to make the decision through consultation, with a group, or by delegation.*
- *If the majority of your responses are "Yes," group decision making may be preferable.*
- *If the majority of your responses are "No," individual decision making may be preferable.*

Question	Yes	No
1. Do you have a reasonable amount of time to make the decision?	☐	☐
2. Does the leader have enough expertise to make a good decision?	☐	☐
3. Do the potential group members have enough expertise to make a good decision?	☐	☐
4. Do the others involved share the organizational goals to be attained by solving the problem?	☐	☐
5. Is the decision complex with many possible solutions?	☐	☐
6. Is commitment to the decision by other people critical?	☐	☐
7. Is the decision likely to cause serious conflict among the people affected by it?	☐	☐
8. Will the decision directly impact many agencies, individuals, or community members?	☐	☐
9. Will the decision directly impact only a select few?	☐	☐

Successful Group Decision Making

Group decision making requires good leadership to be successful. There are special conditions necessary for group decision making, such as adequate time. There are also particular pitfalls unique to group decision making, such as "groupthink."

Avoiding "Groupthink"

"Groupthink" is a phenomenon that occurs in a cohesive group when members let their need to agree with each other interfere with their ability to think about the decision critically.

Three conditions may lead to "groupthink":

1. Overestimation of the group's ability and power:

   - Allows members to ignore warning signals.
   - Allows members to feel complacent.
   - Could result from an overreaction to low self-esteem resulting from recent failures or a difficult task.

2. A "we" vs. "they" attitude:

   - Leads to stereotypes of outsiders.
   - Encourages rationalization of decisions.

3. Pressure toward conformity:

   - Could result from direct pressure applied by the group to members who try to disagree.
   - Does result in members censoring themselves to maintain their membership in the group.

Successful Group Decision Making (Continued)

The key to avoiding or mitigating groupthink lies in the behavior of the group leader. If you are the leader of a group with the potential to exhibit groupthink behavior, you may want to take one or more of the following preventive actions:

- Encourage everyone to air objections and doubts and to accept criticism.

- Describe the problem without revealing your preferred solution.

- Assign the group into subgroups and ask each to evaluate the problem.

- Invite outside experts to challenge the group's decision.

- Ask members to take turns playing "devil's advocate."

Groupthink is more likely to occur in an emergency situation for two reasons:

- Time pressure creates a need for quick decisions.

- Personnel responding to disasters typically have a high degree of cohesion.

To minimize groupthink during an emergency:

- Encourage dissenting opinions consistently.

- Discuss the need to remain open to possibilities with responding personnel *before* an emergency.

- Examine patterns of decision making during previous emergencies and analyze them to take corrective measures.

When leaders can influence their groups to avoid groupthink, decision making becomes possible based on a healthy consensus. Consensus is not the same as 100-percent agreement. In consensus, group members determine that they actively support the decision of the group, even though it might not be their personal choice.

Use Job Aid 3-2, on the following page, to lead groups toward reaching a healthy consensus rather than a premature decision born out of groupthink.

Job Aid 3-2: Reaching Consensus

Use this job aid as a guide to knowing when you've reached consensus and to facilitate gaining consensus from your group.

How do you know when you've reached consensus?

You've reached consensus when each member can say:

- "My personal views and ideas have been really listened to and considered."

- "I have openly listened to and considered the ideas and views of every other group member."

- "I can support this decision and work toward its implementation, even if it was not my choice."

Tips for reaching consensus

- Don't employ win/lose techniques, such as voting or negotiating favors back and forth.

- Look for alternatives that are next most acceptable as ways to break a stalemate.

- Don't encourage members to give in to keep harmony.

Activity: Individual or Group Decision?

This activity will provide you with an opportunity to review several scenarios and determine what type of decision-making process would be most effective. Follow the steps below to complete this activity.

1. Read each of the following scenarios.

2. After reading each scenario, decide whether an individual or group decision would be most appropriate under the circumstances.

3. Give the rationale for your decision.

Scenario 1: Chlorine Truck Accident

You are the emergency manager for Perry County, Pennsylvania, a rural county near Harrisburg, PA. You have just been notified that a truck loaded with liquid chlorine has overturned along State Route 15 at New Buffalo. State Route 15 runs in a north-south direction along the Susquehanna River and is heavily traveled by trucks. New Buffalo is a small town of approximately 400 on the western shore of the Susquehanna. Two miles to the southeast of New Buffalo lies another small town, Amity Hall.

The temperature today is 85 degrees and the wind is blowing from the northeast at 10 miles per hour, gusting to 15 miles per hour.

You are not sure if the truck container is leaking but need to make a decision about whether to evacuate the area under a possible chlorine plume.

1. How should this decision be made?

2. What is your rationale for selecting this decision-making process?

Activity: Individual or Group Decision? (Continued)

Scenario 2: Shelter Planning

You are the shelter coordinator for the local American Red Cross chapter. It is January, and you are beginning the process of reevaluating sheltering needs for the community before hurricane season begins. As part of the process, you have asked all of the shelter managers, the local school superintendent, and personnel from local churches and nursing homes to attend a meeting to review potential shelter locations and capabilities.

1. How should the decision of shelter selection be made?

2. What is your rationale for selecting this decision-making process?

Activity: Individual or Group Decision? (Continued)

Scenario 3: To Sandbag or Not?

It has been raining for 4 days, and the weather forecast is calling for the rain to continue for at least several more days. The river is rising, but is not expected to crest for several more days. Just how high the river will crest is unknown as the rain continues to fall. The director of Public Works has advised you that he doesn't think that sandbags will be effective along the local levee, and has suggested that the area be evacuated. Community groups, however, are concerned about their property and are spontaneously gathering to fill sandbags to add support to the levee. In an effort to gather all information available from all parties, you have called a meeting of the heads of primary response agencies and the community group leaders.

1. How should this decision be made?

2. What is your rationale for selecting this decision-making process?

Activity: Individual or Group Decision? (Continued)

Answers to Scenario 1

If you determined that the decision on what to do in the chlorine emergency is individual decision making, you are correct. Unless information is available immediately, there is no time to gather input from responders before the wind carries the chlorine gas to Amity Hall. Given the weather conditions and the toxicity of chlorine, a decision must be made immediately.

Answers to Scenario 2

There are two possible correct answers for this scenario, depending on the assumptions you made as you read. For example, if you determined that the decision about shelter locations should be made individually through consultation or through group decision making, you are correct. Ultimately, the Red Cross shelter coordinator will be responsible for shelter selection. Therefore, he or she could quite reasonably gather all of the necessary information, then select the shelters. If, however, there are additional factors that make it important to gain the group's agreement on shelter selection, a group decision-making process might be preferable. The decision clearly will not be made individually, because the shelter coordinator has called a meeting. It is also unlikely that the decision would be delegated.

Answers to Scenario 3

If you determined that the decision of whether or not to allow sandbagging would be made through consultation, you are correct. There are clearly too many stakeholders to make the decision individually. On the other hand, because the safety of the citizenry and first responders is at stake, the decision ultimately belongs to the emergency manager. Because there is some time available before a decision has to be made—and because tensions are running high—it is best to get input from first responders and key stakeholders (i.e., the community groups) before making a decision based on the facts of the situation.

What Is an Effective Decision Maker?

Think of someone you know who seems to be a born decision maker. What makes him or her effective? Most likely:

- He or she makes decisions with competence and confidence.

- Most of his or her decisions work out right.

But what is underlying that decision-making skill? Research has shown that effective decision makers share several attributes.

Attributes of an Effective Decision Maker

Effective decision makers tend to have the following attributes:

- **Knowledge.** The most important requirement for making sound decisions is a deep understanding of all factors. The soundness of the decision depends on how informed the decision maker is.

- **Initiative.** Effective decision makers assume responsibility for beginning the decision-making process and seeing it through. They take an active part in making things better.

- **Advice-seeking.** Good decision makers know that they need help from others. They identify people who can make specific contributions to the decision-making process and ask them for their advice and counsel.

- **Selectivity.** Effective decision makers seek pertinent data. They avoid getting bogged down by extraneous facts and figures.

- **Comprehensiveness.** On the other hand, they look at all available options and consider every possible alternative so as to make the best choice.

- **Currency.** Good decision makers consider current conditions and take advantage of opportunities that exist at the time.

- **Flexibility.** Effective decision makers remain open-minded about new concepts and ideas. They are willing to change course or try a different approach if better results seem likely.

- **Good judgment.** Sound decisions will not always result from merely following procedures. Decision makers must exercise their best judgment in considering factors particular to the situation.

Attributes of an Effective Decision Maker (Continued)

- **Calculated risk-taking.** The risks and results of various alternatives must be weighed and the consequences accepted, whether positive or negative.

- **Self-knowledge.** Good decision makers know their own abilities, biases, and limitations.

In addition, smart decision makers will begin with a review of the information at hand (e.g., the EOP, SOPs, etc.) because, if the planning process is complete, many common situations will have been anticipated, and procedures for what to do in those situations will be in place.

Activity: Identifying Your Strengths and Limitations

Write your answers to the questions below in the space provided.

1. In light of your type identified in Unit 3 and the list of attributes of effective decision makers, list your own strengths and weaknesses with respect to decision making.

    Strengths:

    Weaknesses:

2. Keeping in mind that the attributes of effective decision makers can be learned, develop a strategy for using your strengths more fully and minimizing your limitations in decision making. (For example, ask yourself the questions of other dominant modes, or team with others whose strengths complement your weaknesses for group decisions.)

Summary and Transition

Unit 3 reviewed various styles and ways of making decisions and attributes of effective decision makers. Unit 4 discusses ethical decision making.

Knowledge Check

Select the best response. Then, check your answers against the answer key that follows.

1. All of the following are preferred functions for decision making <u>except</u>:

   a. Sensing
   b. Intuition
   c. Acting
   d. Thinking
   e. Feeling

2. The bias in sensing is toward:

   a. Stability
   b. Innovation
   c. Effectiveness
   d. Integrity

3. People organize information by:

   a. Sensing or intuiting
   b. Thinking or feeling

4. The styles of decision making include all of the following <u>except</u>:

   a. Individual
   b. Consultation
   c. Group
   d. Corrective
   e. Delegation

5. In "groupthink," group decision makers:

   a. Reach consensus
   b. Respect everyone's opinion
   c. Are pressured to conform and reach a premature decision
   d. Encourage dissension

Knowledge Check (Continued)

Match the attribute in first column with the description in the second column. Then, turn the page to check your answers.

6. _____ Knowledge

7. _____ Advice-seeking

8. _____ Comprehensiveness

9. _____ Flexibility

10. _____ Calculated risk-taking

a. Effective decision makers remain open-minded about new concepts and ideas. They are willing to change course or try a different approach if better results seem likely.

b. The most important requirement for making sound decisions is a deep understanding of all factors. The soundness of the decision depends on how informed the decision maker is.

c. Good decision makers look at all available options and consider every possible alternative so as to make the best choice.

d. The risks and results of various alternatives must be weighed and the consequences accepted, whether positive or negative.

e. Good decision makers know that they need help from others. They identify people who can make specific contributions to the decision-making process and ask them for their advice and counsel.

Knowledge Check (Continued)

1. c
2. a
3. b
4. d
5. c
6. b
7. e
8. c
9. a
10. d

Unit 4: Ethical Decision Making and Problem Solving

Introduction

In this unit, you will explore what it means to make ethical decisions. After completing this unit, you should be able to:

- Identify potential ethical issues that can arise during an emergency.

- Describe the components of ethical decision making.

- Apply the problem-solving model to ethical issues.

What Is Ethics?

As an emergency management professional, you represent your organization and your profession. Your actions must instill trust and confidence in those with whom you work and in those who depend on you for assistance. In an emergency, victims and coworkers must be able to count on you to carry out your responsibilities in a professional and fair manner.

What's at Issue?

What is at issue in ethical situations arising from emergencies is your personal reputation, your agency's reputation, and ultimately, the public's trust in local government's ability to do the right thing. Also, it is not enough to do the right thing. Public officials must avoid even the appearance of impropriety.

Definition of Ethics

Ethics is a set of standards that guides our behavior, both as individuals and as members of organizations. The ethical principles for this discussion are simple standards of right and wrong that we learn as children, such as being honest and fair and treating others with respect.

Ethical Don'ts

The following "don'ts" address specific ethical challenges in a crisis or emergency situation.

- Don't exceed your authority or make promises.

- Don't use your position to seek personal gain. Examples of seeking personal gain would include:

  - Soliciting gifts.
  - Making official decisions that benefit you financially.
  - Using inside information gained through your position to benefit you and/or your family.
  - Using agency time or property (e.g., a phone or car) for personal reasons.
  - Using your official position or accepting compensation to endorse a product.

Avoid even the appearance of ethical violations. Take the extra step of making sure that your actions (even if they are above-board) could not be seen as unethical. Think about how your actions would read on the front page of the newspaper.

Ethical Do's

Keep these "do's" in mind:

- Place the law and ethical principles above private gain.

- Act impartially. Do not show favoritism to one group (e.g., victims or contractors) over another. Two aids in acting impartially include making sure that all affected parties have full disclosure, and seeking prior authorization before taking action.

- Protect and conserve agency property. This standard applies both to your actions and to the actions that you should take if you observe fraud, waste, or abuse.

- Put forth an honest effort in everything even remotely connected to your official position.

Ethical Issues and Emergencies

Decisions that seem simple or routine in a day-to-day context may become difficult and have serious ethical implications during an emergency. Furthermore, a poor decision with ethical implications can escalate an emergency into an unmanageable situation as the emergency response progresses, as the following scenarios illustrate.

Activity: Ethical Issues and Emergencies

This activity will provide an opportunity for you to examine some of the ethical issues that can arise during an emergency. Follow the steps below to complete this activity:

1. *Read the scenarios that follow.*

2. *Answer the questions that follow each scenario.*

Scenario 1: Train Derailment

On April 17, a train carrying more than 25 propane tankers derailed and began to burn. Upon arriving at the scene and conducting an initial size-up, the incident commander ordered an immediate evacuation of the community, telling evacuees to expect the evacuation to last not more than 2 or 3 hours. As the expected evacuation period was short, some people evacuated without their pets. Electricity was turned off to the area. After 4 hours, the incident commander, in consultation with EOC personnel and chemical experts, determined that the evacuation should continue until the fire burned out.

What are the ethical issues involved in this scenario?

Activity: Ethical Issues and Emergencies (Continued)

Scenario 2: Nuclear Power Plant Fire

You are the emergency manager for Powell County, Arizona. You have just been notified that there is a fire burning inside one of the reactor buildings at a local nuclear power facility. The plant manager has assured you that the fire will not cause a radiation release. However, several persons have been injured, and local emergency personnel are responding. The plant is currently on alert and is considering going to a site area emergency.

The nuclear facility is located 5 miles outside of the Navajo reservation. If there *is* a radiation leak, the wind will carry the radiation across the reservation.

What are the ethical considerations in this scenario?

Activity: Ethical Issues and Emergencies (Continued)

Answers to Scenario 1: Train Derailment

There are several ethical considerations in this scenario.

- Did the incident commander do the right thing by ordering an immediate evacuation? Or should he have waited for more information before issuing the order?
- What should the citizens be told about how long they will be out of their homes?
- Given the current level of risk, can the incident commander ethically allow them to return for their pets?

Answers to Scenario 2: Nuclear Power Plant Fire

Again, several ethical issues are raised by this scenario:

- What should the Navajo tribal leaders be told? Should they be told anything if the fire cannot cause a release?
- Should those living on the reservation shelter in place? Or should they evacuate?
- What about others who may be traveling in the area? Should traffic be rerouted to avoid possible fallout?

You may have identified additional ethical issues for each of these scenarios.

Components of Ethical Decision Making

Ethical decision making requires being aware of your own and your agency's ethical values and applying them whenever necessary. It involves being sensitive to the impact of your decisions and being able to evaluate complex, ambiguous, and/or incomplete facts. Three components of ethical decision making are:

- Commitment

- Consciousness

- Competency

Ethical Commitment

Ethical commitment (or *motivation*) involves demonstrating a strong desire to act ethically and to do the right thing, especially when ethics imposes financial, social, or psychological costs. A crisis or emergency confronts us with many situations that test ethical commitment. Thus, you need to be very clear about your own ethical values and have a strong understanding of ethical standards of conduct.

Ethical Consciousness

Ethical consciousness (or *awareness*) involves seeing and understanding the ethical implications of our behavior and applying our ethical values to our daily lives. Understand that people's perceptions are their reality—and so what we understand to be perfectly legal conduct may be perceived by taxpayers as improper or inappropriate.

Ethical Competency

Ethical competency (or *skill*) involves being competent in ethical decision-making skills, which include:

- **Evaluation.** The ability to collect and evaluate relevant facts, and knowing when to stop collecting facts and to make prudent decisions based on incomplete and ambiguous facts.

- **Creativity.** The capacity to develop resourceful means of accomplishing goals in ways that avoid or minimize ethical problems.

- **Prediction.** The ability to foresee the potential consequences of conduct and assess the likelihood or risk that persons will be helped or harmed by an act.

Applying the Problem-Solving Model to Ethical Issues

Think for a moment about the problem-solving model discussed in Unit 2 and reexamine it in light of what you've just learned about ethics. During Step 3, when selecting an alternative, you should eliminate any alternatives that are unethical—or even give the appearance of being unethical.

In the next activity, you will have an opportunity to apply ethical decision making using the problem-solving model.

Activity: Applying the Problem-Solving Model to Ethical Issues

This activity will provide you with an opportunity to apply the problem-solving model to the ethical issues that arise during emergencies. Follow the steps below to complete this activity:

1. *Read the scenario below.*

2. *Apply the problem-solving model to make decisions about what might have been done in this situation.*

3. *Take time to jot down the rationale for your decisions.*

Flash Flood

The Big Thompson River starts high in the Rocky Mountains and flows eastward down the eastern side of the Continental Divide. Much of the Big Thompson Canyon is steep-walled and rugged. From its source near Estes Park, Colorado, to its mouth, west of Loveland, the Big Thompson drops more than one-half mile.

On Saturday, July 31, 1976, the weather around the Big Thompson Canyon was beautiful, with a small chance of an afternoon or evening thunderstorm. Because 1976 marked Colorado's 100th anniversary of statehood, a large crowd, estimated at between 2,500 and 3,000 people, was at, or driving toward, Big Thompson Canyon.

Late in the afternoon, a thunderstorm formed over the headwaters of the Big Thompson River. By about 6:00 p.m., the storm was dumping heavy rain on the area. The storm remained stationary for 3 hours, dropping more than a foot of rain—eight inches falling during one 2-hour period.

The heavy rain quickly filled the river, turning its typical two-foot-deep flow into a wall of water 19 feet high. As the water raced downstream, it destroyed everything in its path—recreation and commercial buildings, homes, and U.S. Highway 34, which was the only road from which to exit the canyon.

Activity: Applying the Problem-Solving Model to Ethical Issues (Continued)

Flash Flood (Continued)

Use the problem-solving model to answer the questions below. Assume that you are the Emergency Manager.

1. Would you send anyone up the canyon to warn others? Why or why not?

2. What is your ethical responsibility to the public and to responders?

 **Activity: Applying the Problem-Solving Model to Ethical Issues (Continued)**

Answers to Flash Flood Scenario

There are no "right" or "wrong" answers to this case. Your answers are correct if they:

- Represent the best option from the alternatives you developed.
- Are feasible.
- Are ethical.

Summary and Transition

In Unit 4, you examined ethical decision making and problem solving. In Unit 5, you will apply the problem-solving model to a case study.

For More Information

Alsott, J.D. The Search for Honor: An Inquiry Into the Factors That Influence the Ethics of Federal Acquisition. In J.A. Petrick, W.M. Claunch, & R.F. Scherer (Eds.), *Institutionalizing Organizational Ethics Programs: Contemporary Perspectives* (pp. 182-194). Dayton, OH: Wright State University, 1991.

Atwood, D.J. Living up to the public trust. *Defense Issues,* Vol. 5, 1990, p. 1.

Crawford, S.J. III Wind and Well-learned Lessons. *Defense,* Vol. 90, July-August 1990, p. 15.

Josephson, M. *Making Ethical Decisions.* The Josephson Institute of Ethics, 1992, 1993.

Karp, H.B. & Abramms, B. Doing the Right Thing. *Training and Development,* August 1992, pp. 37-41.

Executive Order 12731, Principles of Ethical Conduct for Government Officers and Employees. *Federal Register,* Vol. 55, No. 203, October 19, 1990, Presidential Documents.

Government Ethics Center of the Joseph and Edna Josephson Institute of Ethics. *Ethics at the IRS: A Quest for the Highest Standards* (Internal Revenue Service Management Training Program: Workshop and Resource Materials). Marina Del Rey, CA, 1991.

Knowledge Check

Select the best response. Then, turn the page to check your answers.

1. If you are sure you have acted ethically, you should not be concerned with how your actions appear to others.

   a. True
   b. False

2. All of the following are examples of using your position to seek personal gain except:

   a. Soliciting gifts
   b. Exceeding your authority or making promises
   c. Using inside information
   d. Using agency time or property

3. The components of ethical decision making include all of the following except:

   a. Motivation
   b. Awareness
   c. Intuition
   d. Skill

4. Ethical competency consists of all of the following except:

   a. Judgment
   b. Evaluation
   c. Creativity
   d. Prediction

5. Another name for ethical commitment is:

   a. Awareness
   b. Skill
   c. Consciousness
   d. Motivation

Knowledge Check (Continued)

1. b
2. b
3. c
4. a
5. d

Unit 5: Decision Making in an Emergency

Introduction

In this unit, you will examine the effect of stress on decision making and apply the problem-solving model to a case study. At the end of this unit, you should be able to make decisions and solve the problems described in the case study.

Decision Making and Stress

Decisions can be as simple as delegating a routine task or as complex as responding to a major crisis. Decision making in a crisis is made more difficult because of stress.

Impediments to making good decisions under stress include:

- Perceived or real time pressure.

- Possible political pressures.

- High- or low-blood sugar levels as a result of erratic eating patterns.

- Caffeine.

- Sleep deprivation and resulting fatigue.

- Lack of information.

- Conflicting information.

- Uncertainty.

Under stress, decision makers are more likely to:

- Experience conflict with other key players.

- Perceive selectively because of sensory overload, and thus perhaps miss important information.

- Experience perception distortion and poor judgment.

Decision Making and Stress (Continued)

Decision makers under stress also tend to:

- Be less tolerant of ambiguity and thus perhaps make premature decisions.

- Experience a decreased ability to handle difficult tasks and work productively.

- Experience a greater tendency toward aggression and escape behaviors.

They may also:

- Consider only immediate survival goals, sacrificing long-range considerations.

- Choose a risky alternative.

- Get tunnel vision.

- Succumb to "groupthink."

An important key to effective decision making in a crisis is being systematic. A good way to be systematic is to use the problem-solving model.

Case Study: Hurricane Hortence

Read the following case study and updates and answer the questions that follow.

North Carolina: September 5, 2002

Hurricane Hortence slammed into North Carolina's southern coast on September 5, 2002, with sustained winds of approximately 115 miles per hour and gusts as high as 125 miles per hour. At some point, 1.7 million customers in North Carolina lost electricity. Traveling in the wake of Hurricane Frank, which struck the same area in July, Hortence's 12-foot storm surge caused extensive damage from the South Carolina border to Surf City, NC.

Hortence had become a tropical depression on August 24, then weakened before strengthening again into a minimal hurricane on August 29 as it threatened the Lesser Antilles. After bypassing the Lesser Antilles, Hortence weakened to a tropical storm, then strengthened again as it neared the Bahamas. As Hortence approached the U.S. coast, it had hurricane-force winds extending as far as 140 miles from the storm center.

You are the Emergency Manager for Brunswick County, NC, which includes Wilmington. The main roads out of the Wilmington area run east-west, but evacuees need to head north. It is Labor Day weekend, and approximately 350,000 people need to be evacuated.

1. Given Hortence's history of weakening, then strengthening, at what point would you open the EOC and notify response personnel?

2. What decision would you recommend concerning issuing a mandatory evacuation order? How would you proceed with the evacuation (if one is ordered)? Why?

3. What would you tell those citizens who decide to shelter in place? What would you tell responders?

4. What potential problems do you foresee in the scenario that you would have made contingency plans for?

Case Study: Hurricane Hortence (Continued)

10:30 A.M. EDT, September 6, 2002

Hortence made landfall during the night of September 5. Damage in the Wilmington and surrounding areas is severe. Initial damage assessment indicates that the water treatment facility has been breached by flood waters; tornadoes have damaged power lines throughout the area; and the storm surge has carried homes, businesses, and churches off their foundations. It is clear that many of those in shelters will be unable to return to their homes in the foreseeable future.

Calls are coming in via cellular phone requesting emergency rescue of citizens who ignored the evacuation order and decided to shelter in place. Because cell phone locations take longer to pinpoint, these calls, together with other emergency calls, are jamming the 9-1-1 lines.

Also, because water levels remain high and electricity is out through most of the area, much of the public is unaware of the severity of the damage. Many are anxious to return to their homes.

5. What steps would you take to notify the public of the current level of risk?

6. What would you do to correct the communications problem at the 9-1-1 center?

7. What potential problems do you foresee in the scenario that you would have made contingency plans for?

Case Study: Hurricane Hortence (Continued)

12:15 P.M., September 6, 2002

An elderly couple requiring an emergency rescue has refused to leave without their cat. Flood waters have surrounded their house to the second floor. The water rescue team reports that the house is unstable.

A fire has broken out in the center of Wilmington. Because the water levels remain high, firefighters are unable to approach the blaze.

Before the hurricane season began, shelters were stocked with supplies for 3 days, based on 100-percent capacity. Most shelters are currently over their capacity—some by as much as 50 percent. Some shelters will have to remain open for the foreseeable future.

8. What would you tell the elderly couple? The rescuers?

9. How would you deal with the fire?

10. What would you do to resolve the pending issues at the shelters?

Case Study: Hurricane Hortence (Continued)

Answers to Case Study

1. Given Hortence's history of weakening, then strengthening, at what point would you open the EOC and notify response personnel?

   Hortence has weakened and strengthened several times since August 24. However, at the time of this case study, it is a Category 3 storm. Also:

   - It is Labor Day weekend, and the number of evacuees is much greater than it would otherwise be.
   - There is an obvious transportation problem, as the main routes out of Brunswick County follow the projected path of the hurricane.

   Given the problems (i.e., large numbers of evacuees needing to head north, not west or northwest), alternatives may be limited. The obvious first place to look is the Hurricane Appendix of the EOP, which should include a Time Delineating Schedule (TDS) that provides a timeline for all key actions in preparation for a hurricane. If a TDS is part of the Hurricane Appendix, it should provide the timeframes for EOC opening and personnel notification. If not, alternatives and a solution can be derived from histories of similar storms and inundation maps of the area. However, time is short to be gathering data at this point.

2. What decision would you recommend concerning issuing a mandatory evacuation order? How would you proceed with the evacuation (if one is ordered)? Why?

   Given the size of the storm, a mandatory evacuation is required. If the Hurricane Appendix includes a TDS, the timeframe for issuance should be included. If not, the logical way to proceed would be by issuing a mandatory evacuation order, beginning with islands and low-lying coastal areas.

Case Study: Hurricane Hortence (Continued)

Answers to Case Study (Continued)

3. What would you tell the citizens who decide to shelter in place? What would you tell responders?

    The answer to this question may depend on State law. (Some States do not have the authority to require an evacuation.) However, citizens who shelter in place pose risks, not only to themselves, but to response personnel who may be required to rescue them later when the risk has increased dramatically. Obviously, the goal is to have everyone evacuate. Alternatives may include (but may not be limited to):

    *   Doing nothing and leaving those who wish to shelter in place to their own devices.
    *   Using the Emergency Alert System (EAS), public service announcements (PSAs), local newscasts, etc., to emphasize the risk that those who shelter in place are taking.
    *   Forcibly removing the persons.

    Of those options, the only option that is both ethical and will not cause ill will at the time or later is to use EAS, PSA, news, and other methods to emphasize the seriousness of the situation. Given the seriousness of the situation, the other issues that must be addressed, and the timeframes in which decisions must be made, there may be little else to do. Unfortunately, evaluating the solution may come at a time when it is too late and lives have been lost.

    What you tell responders may depend on your decision on those who shelter in place. One point is for certain, however. Responders will be unable to help anyone if they are injured. Whatever decision you make must take the level of risk to response personnel into consideration.

4. What potential problems do you foresee in this scenario that you would have made contingency plans for?

    There are several potential problems that may require contingency plans. Because of the increased number of evacuees:

    *   More time may be required for evacuation than is provided in the TDS. (Don't forget that adjacent areas along the coast are also evacuating.)
    *   Additional shelters may have to be opened, and additional supplies may be required.
    *   Plans may need to be made for search and rescue operations following the storm.
    *   Plans may need to be made for vector control following the storm.
    *   Plans will need to be made to ensure that water is available and safe.

    You probably have foreseen other problems requiring contingencies as well.

Case Study: Hurricane Hortence (Continued)

Answers to Case Study (Continued)

5. What steps would you take to notify the public of the current level of risk?

   Even though electricity is out to much of the area, it is still possible much of the public can be reached through the usual methods (e.g., EAS, news broadcasts, etc.). In addition, the following may be options:

   - Using RACES operators to broadcast information about current conditions and level of risk.
   - Emergency communications (either via radio, cell phone, or in person) should be made with all shelters to provide information and warn evacuees to remain at the shelters.
   - Where possible, public address systems (either on emergency vehicles or boats) could be used to provide information about the situation.

6. What would you do to correct the communications problem at the 9-1-1 center?

   The answer to this question depends on the communications capability in Brunswick County. It may be possible, however, to switch some calls to another temporary call center or to add additional temporary lines.

7. What potential problems do you foresee in the scenario that you would have made contingency plans for?

   The most obvious issues for which contingency plans must be prepared are:

   - Vector control.
   - Long-range sheltering.
   - Emergency restoration of utilities and other lifelines.

   You may have identified other issues as well.

8. What would you tell the elderly couple? The rescuers?

   While the elderly couple are attached to their cat, human life (both the couple's and the rescuers') must take priority. An initial strategy (assuming that the cat cannot be found quickly) is to quickly explain the danger that the couple is in and the fact that they must leave their home. Hopefully, they will see reason and cooperate. It's entirely possible, however, that because of the age of the couple and the stress of the situation, the rescuers may need to forcibly evacuate them.

Case Study: Hurricane Hortence (Continued)

Answers to Case Study (Continued)

9. How would you deal with the fire?

   The answer to this question depends on what resources are available, where they are located, and what the operational priorities are. It may be necessary merely to try to contain the fire using minimal resources.

10. What would you do to resolve the pending issues at the shelters?

   This question has both short- and long-term implications. The immediate need is for additional supplies and, perhaps, additional shelters. The longer-range need is to provide long-term shelters for those who have been permanently displaced by the storm. In either case, consultation with personnel from the American Red Cross, other Voluntary Agencies Active in Disaster (VOAD) members, and local service providers would be called for. At that meeting, you could gather the information required, discuss options, and select a solution that is the most reasonable and workable for all involved.

Summary and Transition

In Unit 5, you examined the effect of stress on decision making and applied the problem-solving model to a case study. Unit 6 will summarize the course content and include the Final Exam.

Unit 6: Course Summary

Introduction

This unit will summarize the key points of the course.

The Decision-Making Process

Problem solving is a set of activities designed to analyze a situation systematically and find, implement, and evaluate solutions.

Decision making is making choices at each step of the problem-solving process.

The emergency decision-making process begins well before disaster strikes. EOPs and SOPs provide the foundation for decision making during emergencies.

The Problem-Solving Model

The problem-solving model that is used for this course contains five steps.

1. **Identify the problem.** This step includes delineating the problem parameters such as:

   - What is happening (and not happening).
   - Who is involved.
   - What is at stake.

2. **Explore alternatives.** This step includes two parts:

   - Generating alternatives through brainstorming, surveys, or discussion groups.
   - Evaluating alternatives.

3. **Select an alternative.**

4. **Implement the solution.** This step includes five parts:

   - Develop an action plan.
   - Determine objectives.
   - Identify needed resources.
   - Build a plan.
   - Implement the plan.

5. **Evaluate the situation.** This step includes two parts:

   - Monitoring progress.
   - Evaluating the results.

Factors that affect decision making include:

- Political factors.

- Safety factors.

- Financial factors.

- Environmental factors.

- Ethical factors.

Decision-Making Styles

People have different styles of making decisions that depend on their personality or psychological type. Psychological type is a composite of our preferences, or preferred ways of taking in and organizing information. We tend to favor one of four ways of approaching a problem:

- Sensing (stability)

- Intuition (innovation)

- Thinking (effectiveness)

- Feeling (integrity)

Although each approach has its strengths, each also has its blind spots. It is helpful to learn to ask the questions that all four approaches ask so as to arrive at more considered and, therefore, sounder decisions.

Decisions can also be made in one of four styles, depending on who is making the decision:

- Individual

- Consultation

- Group

- Delegation

An important consideration in group decision making is avoiding "groupthink", in which group pressure produces a premature decision.

Attributes of an Effective Decision Maker

Effective decision makers tend to have the following ten characteristics:

- Knowledge

- Initiative

- Advice-seeking

- Selectivity

- Comprehensiveness

- Currency

- Flexibility

- Good judgment

- Calculated risk-taking

- Self-knowledge

Ethical Decision Making

Ethics are a set of standards such as honesty, respect, and fairness that guide behavior. In the emergency management profession, ethical behavior is critical because disaster victims and coworkers must be able to depend on you.

Ethical "don'ts" include:

- Don't exceed your authority or make promises.

- Don't use your position for personal gain.

- Avoid even the appearance of ethical violations.

Ethical "do's" include:

- Place the law and principle above private gain.

- Act impartially.

- Protect and conserve agency property.

- Put forth honest effort.

Ethical decision making has three components:

- Commitment or motivation

- Consciousness or awareness

- Competency or skill

Apply ethics to the problem-solving model. It is important in Step 3, selecting alternatives, to eliminate any alternatives that are unethical or give the appearance of being so.

The Final Step

You have now completed IS 241 and should be ready to take the final exam.

Complete the final exam in the back of the book by marking the correct responses.

To submit the final exam online, to http://training.fema.gov/IS and click on the courses link. Click on the title for this course, and scroll down the course description page to locate the final exam link. After you have selected the final exam link and the online answer sheet is open, transfer your answers, and complete the personal identification data requested.

To submit the final exam by mail using the standard answer sheet, follow the instructions printed on the form.

Good luck!

Appendix: Job Aids

Step 1 Job Aid: Checklist for Identifying, Defining, and Analyzing Problems

Question	Yes	No
1. Is this a new problem?	☐	☐
2. Is the problem clearly and precisely stated?	☐	☐
3. What assumptions am I making about the problem? Are they true?	☐	☐
4. What would happen if <u>nothing</u> were done about this problem?		
5. Can the problem be restated in other terms? If yes, how?	☐	☐
6. What <u>data</u> are known that bear on the problem?		

Step 1 Job Aid: Checklist for Identifying, Defining, and Analyzing Problems (Continued)

Question	Yes	No
7. Is the information accurate?	☐	☐
8. Are there any precedents or rules about other procedures that apply to the problem? If so, what precedents or rules apply?	☐	☐
9. What additional facts are needed to analyze the problem? (List)		
10. Is it possible to interpret the facts differently? How would that affect the problem's solution?	☐	☐
11. Do I have to make this decision, or does someone else? If this decision is someone else's to make, whose is it?	☐	☐

Step 2 Job Aid: Criteria for Evaluating Alternatives

Step	Questions to Ask
1. Identify Constraints	Do any of the following factors serve as a limitation on this solution? ■ Technical (limited equipment or technology) ■ Political (legal restrictions or ordinances) ■ Economic (cost or capital restrictions) ■ Social (restrictions imposed by organized groups with special interests) ■ Human resources (limited ability of relevant people to understand or initiate certain actions) ■ Time (requirements that a solution be found within a prescribed time period, thereby eliminating consideration of long-range solutions)
2. Determine Appropriateness	Does this solution fit the circumstances?
3. Verify Adequacy	Will this option make enough of a difference to be worth doing?
4. Evaluate Effectiveness	Will this option meet the objective?
5. Evaluate Efficiency	What is the cost/benefit ratio of this option?
6. Determine Side Effects	What are the ramifications of this option?

Step 3 Job Aid: Best Solutions

Solution:		
Limiting Factors:		
Political:		
Safety:		
Financial:		
Environmental:		
Ethical:		
Other:		

Solution:		
Limiting Factors:		
Political:		
Safety:		
Financial:		
Environmental:		
Ethical:		
Other:		

Solution:		
Limiting Factors:		
Political:		
Safety:		
Financial:		
Environmental:		
Ethical:		
Other:		

If you have more than one clear solution, can any be combined?

Step 4 Job Aid: Action Planning Checklist

Use the following questions to help you develop any details needed to plan for implementation of the decision.

1. Will the decision be implemented as it stands or will it have to be modified?

    ☐ As it stands
    ☐ With modifications (List)

2. Does the decision fit the problem and conditions specified earlier?

    ☐ Yes
    ☐ No

3. Is this still the best option?

    ☐ Yes
    ☐ No

    (If no, what has changed?)

4. What are the side effects of this decision?

5. Who is responsible for taking action?

Step 4 Job Aid: Action Planning Checklist (Continued)

6. Are the specific targets to be accomplished and the techniques for accomplishing them defined?

   ☐ Yes
   ☐ No

   If no, what targets and techniques required further definition?

7. What specific activities must take place to implement this decision? In what sequence?

8. What resources will be needed to implement this decision?

9. What is the schedule or timetable for implementation of each step in the action plan?

Step 5 Job Aid: Checklist for Evaluating the Results

Use the questions below as a guide for evaluating the results of your decision making.

Question	Yes	No
1. How will you know if the proposed decision has worked?		
Is it measurable? If yes, how?	☐	☐
2. Does the decision and action plan make use of existing channels of communication to generate feedback?	☐	☐
3. Will the feedback test the effectiveness of the decision?	☐	☐
4. Will the feedback be sufficient to reflect changing circumstances and conditions that might occasion the need to modify the plan?	☐	☐
5. Is the solution achieving its purpose?	☐	☐
6. Is timely information generated so that it can be supplied to operational, administrative, and policy units in the jurisdiction?	☐	☐

Job Aid 3-1: Selecting a Decision-Making Approach

Use the questions below as a guide to developing a decision-making approach. Answer each of the questions below.

- *If the response to question 1 is "No," it may be preferable to make the decision individually or in consultation with key players.*
- *If the response to question 2 is "No," it may be preferable to make the decision through consultation, with a group, or by delegation.*
- *If the majority of your responses are "Yes," group decision making may be preferable.*
- *If the majority of your responses are "No," individual decision making may be preferable.*

Question	Yes	No
1. Do you have a reasonable amount of time to make the decision?	☐	☐
2. Does the leader have enough expertise to make a good decision?	☐	☐
3. Do the potential group members have enough expertise to make a good decision?	☐	☐
4. Do the others involved share the organizational goals to be attained by solving the problem?	☐	☐
5. Is the decision complex with many possible solutions?	☐	☐
6. Is commitment to the decision by other people critical?	☐	☐
7. Is the decision likely to cause serious conflict among the people affected by it?	☐	☐
8. Will the decision directly impact many agencies, individuals, or community members?	☐	☐
9. Will the decision directly impact only a select few?	☐	☐

Job Aid 3-2: Reaching Consensus

Use this job aid as a guide to knowing when you've reached consensus and to facilitate gaining consensus from your group.

How do you know when you've reached consensus?

You've reached consensus when each member can say:

- "My personal views and ideas have been really listened to and considered."

- "I have openly listened to considered the ideas and views of every other group member."

- "I can support this decision and work toward its implementation, even if it was not my choice."

Tips for reaching consensus

- Don't employ win/lose techniques, such as voting or negotiating favors back and forth.

- Look for alternatives that are next most acceptable as ways to break a stalemate.

- Don't encourage members to give in to keep harmony.

www.ingramcontent.com/pod-product-compliance
Lightning Source LLC
Chambersburg PA
CBHW070157290526
45789CB00002B/800